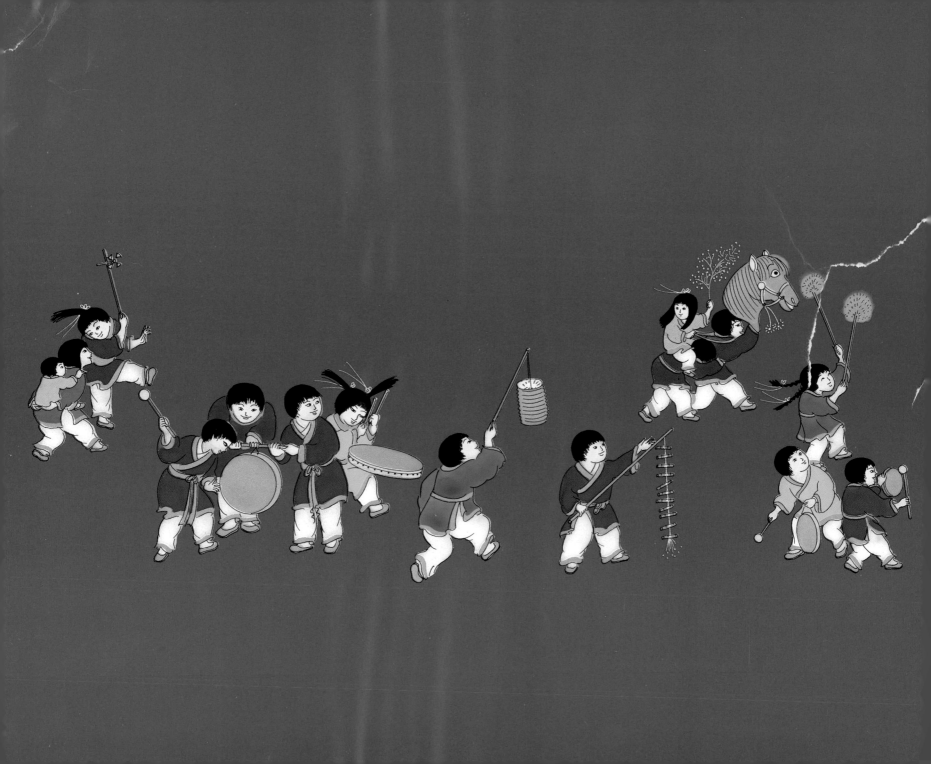

HAPPY NEW YEAR!

DEMI

CROWN PUBLISHERS, INC. ♛ NEW YORK

KUNG-HSI FA-TS'AI!

Published by Crown Publishers, Inc.,
a Random House company,
201 East 50th Street, New York,
New York 10022.

CROWN is a trademark of
Crown Publishers, Inc.

http://www.randomhouse.com/

Printed in Singapore

Library of Congress
Cataloging-in-Publication Data

Demi.

Happy New Year!/Kung-hsi fa-ts'ai!
/by Demi.— 1st ed.
        p.   cm.
Summary: Examines the customs,
traditions, foods, and lore associated
with the celebration of Chinese
New Year.

1. Chinese New Year—Juvenile literature.
2. China—Social life and customs—
Juvenile literature. [1. Chinese New
Year.] I. Title.

GT4905.D45   1998
394.261—dc21   97-11692

ISBN 0-517-70957-0 (trade)
ISBN 0-517-70958-9 (lib. bdg.)

10 9 8 7 6 5 4 3 2

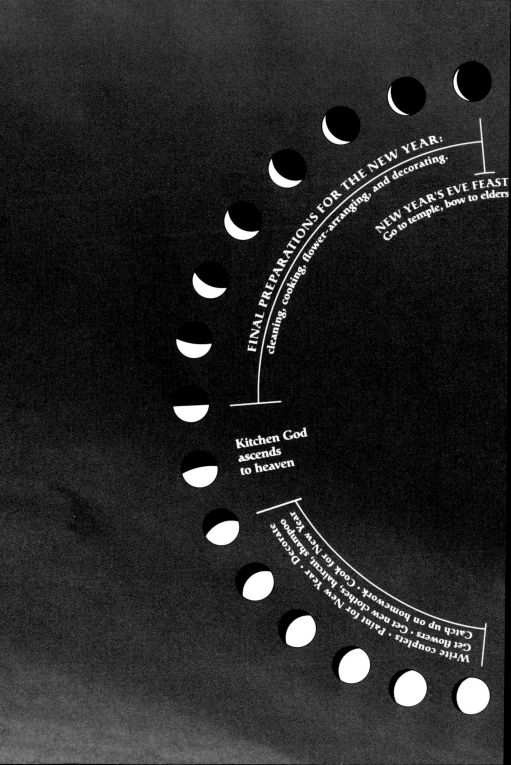

FINAL PREPARATIONS FOR THE NEW YEAR:
cleaning, cooking, flower-arranging, and decorating.

NEW YEAR'S EVE FEAST
Go to temple, bow to elders

Kitchen God
ascends
to heaven

Write couplets · Paint for New Year · Decorate
Get flowers · Get new clothes, haircut, shampoo
Catch up on homework · Cook for New Year

NEW MOON

New Year's Day

HAPPY NEW YEAR!

DRAGON DANCES
LION DANCES
DRAGON DANCES
DRAGON DANCES
DRAGON DANCES
LANTERN FESTIVAL

FULL MOON

THE CHINESE NEW YEAR CELEBRATION

The Chinese New Year is determined by the Chinese lunar calendar. The new year begins with the new moon.

The last fifteen days of the old year are spent preparing for the New Year celebration. That is the time for cleaning the house, cooking special foods for the New Year's Eve feast, and making banners, decorations, and other things to get ready for the celebration.

The first fifteen days of the new year are spent celebrating. There are feasts, dragon dances, lantern festivals, lion dances, and many other festivities to celebrate the new year.

THE ANIMAL ZODIAC

Each Chinese year is named after an animal, and each animal has certain characteristics. Because the moon's cycle begins again every 12 years, there are 12 animals in the Chinese zodiac – one for each year of the lunar cycle.

SNAKES are quiet, deep, and wise! Determined, vain, and intense! Their friends are the Ox and the Rooster, but not the Pig. Snakes are born in the years 1929, 1941, 1953, 1965, 1977, 1989, 2001.

HORSES are popular and cheerful! Independent, quick, and artful! Their friends are the Tiger and the Dog, but not the Rat. Horses are born in the years 1930, 1942, 1954, 1966, 1978, 1990, 2002.

GOATS are religious (for they kneel when they drink), creative, and shy! Elegant, emphatic, and wise! Their friends are the Rabbit and the Pig, but not the Ox. Goats are born in the years 1931, 1943, 1955, 1967, 1979, 1991, 2003.

MONKEYS are smart, skillful, and successful! They are knowledgeable and discriminating! Their friends are the Dragon and the Rat, but not the Tiger. Monkeys are born in the years 1932, 1944, 1956, 1968, 1980, 1992, 2004.

DOGS are loyal, honest, and cooperative! Faithful, confident, and eccentric! Their friends are the Tiger and the Horse, but not the Dragon. Dogs are born in the years 1934, 1946, 1958, 1970, 1982, 1994, 2006.

ROOSTERS are ambitious, hardworking, and adventurous! Deep-thinking, eccentric, and opinionated! Their friends are the Snake and the Ox, but not the Rabbit. Roosters are born in the years 1933, 1945, 1957, 1969, 1981, 1993, 2005.

RABBITS are lucky, virtuous, and reserved!
Talented, affectionate, and long-lived!
Their friends are the Goat and the Pig,
but not the Rooster. Rabbits are born in the years
1927, 1939, 1951, 1963, 1975, 1987, 1999.

DRAGONS are wealthy,
wise, and powerful!
Eccentric, honest, and brave!
Their friends are the Rat and
the Monkey, but not the Dog.
Dragons are born in the years 1928,
1940, 1952, 1964, 1976, 1988, 2000.

TIGERS are powerful, protective, and sympathetic!
Short-tempered, deep-thinking, and courageous!
Their friends are the Horse and the Dog,
but not the Monkey. Tigers are born in the years
1926, 1938, 1950, 1962, 1974, 1986, 1998.

OXEN are patient, confident, and eccentric!
Quiet, strong, and stubborn!
Their friends are the Snake and the Rooster,
but not the Goat. Oxen are born in the years
1937, 1949, 1961, 1973, 1985, 1997, 2009.

RATS are charming, picky, and thrifty!
Ambitious, adventurous, and deep-thinking!
Their friends are the Dragon and the Monkey,
but not the Horse. Rats are born in the years
1936, 1948, 1960, 1972, 1984, 1996, 2008.

PIGS are ambitious, strong, and honest!
Wealthy, studious, and kind!
Their friends are the Rabbit and the Goat,
but not the Snake. Pigs are born in the years
1935, 1947, 1959, 1971, 1983, 1995, 2007.

plow

sow

plant

reap

pound

sift

store

thresh

IT'S SPRING!

The Chinese New Year falls during China's springtime.
(In the Western calendar, Chinese New Year usually takes
place in January or February.) For thousands of years,
China has been an agricultural country, and the people
are in harmony with the seasons and the cycles of planting
and harvesting. The Chinese New Year celebrates the
season for planting, as well as all new beginnings.

SWEEP AND DUST!

Part of getting ready for the Chinese New Year is making sure your home is neat and clean before the new year arrives. Tidy up your house and your room. Sweep out the old and bring in the New Year!

Now is also the time to get new seeds for planting.

mop

dust

scrub

brush

sweep

wash

polish

MAKE A FRESH START!

Wash your hair and get a new haircut. Buy some new clothes.
Pay the debts that you owe and collect what is owed to you!
Catch up on your homework!

DECORATE!

Create New Year wishes and poems about luck, good fortune, and happiness. Write them on banners of red and gold and use them to decorate your house.

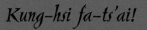

Kung-hsi fa-ts'ai!

Best wishes for great wealth and prosperity!

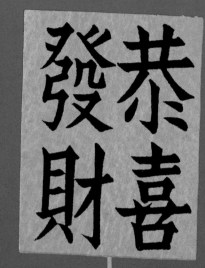

Fu

Magic writing to protect the household.

Chao-ts'ai chin-pao!

May you have wealth and treasures!

Huang-chin wan-liang!

May you have ten thousand pieces of gold!

Fu–lu–shou!

May you have longevity, prosperity, and posterity!

Chao–ts'ai chin–pao!

May you have wealth and treasures!

Hui–ch'un!

May your business have a successful year!

Kung–hsi fa–ts'ai!

All the best for a Happy New Year!

Fooh!

May you have happiness and great fortune!

PAINT AND PARADE!

Children paint pictures of their favorite gods, animals, and symbols and carry them in the streets on New Year's Day!

Ch'in Ch'iung!
The protector from evil!

T'ien-kuan!
Bringer of gifts!

Kuan-yin!
Goddess of mercy!

Chung K'uei!
Guardian of the household!

Kuan Yu!
Symbol of loyalty, integrity, and trustworthiness!

Ts'ai Shen Yeh!
The god of wealth!

Yao-ch'ien-shu!
**The money tree
of great riches!**

*Messenger of
Ts'ai Shen Yeh!*
**Messenger of the
god of wealth!**

Yu Huang Da-ti!
**The ruler of everything
and bringer of sons!**

Shou-hsing!
The star of longevity!

Fu-lu-shou!
**Triple blessings of
happinesss, position,
and longevity!**

Ch'i-lin Sung-tzu!
**The celestial immortal
who brings children!**

COOK!

The New Year festivities include a feast on New Year's Eve. Everyone helps prepare the special foods that will be served. These foods have special meanings and are symbols of what is wished for in the year to come.

New Year's cakes and candies represent — peace and harmony, Chuen-ho.

— Candied melon, Jen, symbolizes wealth, virtue, growth, and good health.

Taffy candy, T'ang-kua, is for the Kitchen God, Tsun Kuan. —

— Mandarin cakes, Sa-ch'i-ma, represent all wishes fulfilled.

Puffed rice cakes, Mi-t'ung, stand for a sweet new year. —

— Pudding cake, Nien-kao, stands for a lucky new year.

Rice dumplings, Chiao-tzu, means good fortune and heavenly blessings. —

— Fried rice symbolizes harmony and plenty, Chao-fan.

Steamed buns, Man-t'ou, stand for good luck and good fortune. —

— Fish symbolizes surplus, Yu.

Oysters represent good fortune, Hao-shih. —

— Clams signify profit and good omens, Hsien.

Shrimp represents wealth and abundance, Hsia. —

— A pair of carp symbolize fame and fortune, Ming-li Shuang Shou.

Sweet-and-sour fish signifies surplus, Ch'o-yu Yu-yu. —

— Pan-fried fish means that luck is coming, Shih-lai Lien-tao.

Beef stands for strengthening powers, Chiao-tzu. —

— Duck represents happiness, Yuan Yang.

Pork brings wealth, K'ou-jou. —

— Chinese cabbage represents wealth, Pai-ts'ai.

Lettuce signifies wealth and riches, Sheng-ts'ai. —

— Seaweed, Fa-ts'ai, means "Happy New Year!"

Persimmons mean that all wishes will be fulfilled, Tang-kuo. —

POP! POP! POP!

Firecrackers are an important part of the
New Year celebration. The firecrackers
are lit in front of each house, and the
loud noises scare away the evil spirits.
When the evil spirits have been scared
away, the door guardians will make
sure that the house is safe.

**The door guardian
Yu-chih Kung,
protector from evil.**

The door guardian
Ch'in Ch'iung,
protector from evil.

BOW AND PRAY

On New Year's Eve, people go to the temple to pray for their ancestors and for good fortune. Children bow and pray and pay respect to parents and elders. No bad words can be said, or you will have bad luck for the new year. On this day, children are given red money bags, called *Li-shih*, so they will prosper and be happy.

Dingguang Fo
DIPANKARA
Buddha of the past

Mimi Fo
AMITAYUS
Buddha of Paradise, Sukhavati

Qing Jing Fo
AMOGHASIDDHI
Buddha who represents perfect wisdom and destroys jealousy

Achu Fo
AKSHOBYA
Buddha who sees clear and destroys anger

Shijiamouni Fo
SHAKYAMUNI
**Buddha of wisdom
and compassion**

Palushena
MAHAVARIOCANA
**Buddha of universal wisdom,
who destroys stupidity**

Baosheng Fo
RATNASAMBHAVA
**Buddha of equality,
who destroys ego**

Mituo Fo
AMITABA
**Buddha of infinite light,
who destroys passions**

Mile Fo
MAITREYA
Buddha of the future

*Heavenly King
Mo-li Shou,*
**Protector of the
North.**

Chang Kuo Lau,
**an invisible immortal
who plays music on
the Yu Ku, a drum
made of bamboo.**

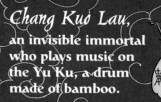

*Heavenly King
Mo-li Hai,*
Protector of the West.

Lan Ts'ai Ho,
**an immortal who
sings and gives to the
poor. Saint of florists.**

Lu Tung Pin,
**an immortal scholar
whose sword destroys
greed, hatred, ignorance,
passion, and jealousy.
Saint of the sick.**

Ho Hsien Ku,
**an immortal who eats
pearls and moonbeams.
Saint of household
government.**

HEAVENLY BEINGS

Heavenly beings are protectors and guardians.
Praying to them will help ensure that the new
year will be a safe, happy, and fruitful one.

*Heavenly K
Mo-li Hung*
**Protector of t
South.**

Li T'ieh Kuai,
an immortal in the
body of a beggar who
uses an iron crutch.

**The Jade Emperor,
Yu Huang Da-ti,**
bestows blessings
according to merit.

Ian Hsiang-tzu,
n immortal who gives
the poor and plays a
ute to Heaven. Saint
f musicians.

Chung-li Chuan,
an immortal scholar
with a fan, who knows
the magic of immortality
and transformation.

Ts'ao Kuo Chiu,
a royal immortal who carried
symbolic royal tablets, which
he discarded to enter Heaven.
Saint of actors.

**The Kitchen God,
Tsun Kuan,**
rises to heaven once a year
to report to the Jade Emperor.
Tsun Kuan tells him how good
you've been throughout the year.

**Heavenly King
Mo-li Ch'ing,**
Protector of the East.

SWEET GIFTS!

New Year's Day is the time to visit family and friends. It is important to bring special gifts like melon seeds, flowers, candied fruit, and New Year's cakes to everyone you visit. Each gift brings with it special symbolic wishes for the coming year.

A tray of candies, called Chuen-ho, represents togetherness.
Candied melon will ensure growth and good health.
Candied lotus seeds will help to bring many sons into the family.
Candied coconut creates togetherness.
New Year rice cakes will sweeten your year.
And a gift of watermelon seeds is a wish for plenitude.

TREES AND FLOWERS!

Flowers and trees play a special part in the New Year. Each tree and flower has a special spiritual meaning and will bring those good things to people who receive them as gifts.

PINE branches symbolize nobility.

PEONY signifies spring, wealth, and bravery.

FUCHSIA represents sweetness and fragrance.

BAMBOO stands for flexibility.

SNAPDRAGONS symbolize instant riches and luck.

SUGARCANE signifies gratitude.

ORANGE and TANGERINE stand for strength and perseverance.

FORSYTHIA symbolizes
happiness and joy.

PEACH stands for wealth.

PLUM represents
strength and temerity.

CYPRESS stands
for plenty.

NARCISSUS represents
divine purity.

ORCHID stands for good
luck and good fortune.

PUSSY WILLOW
represents
prosperity for all.

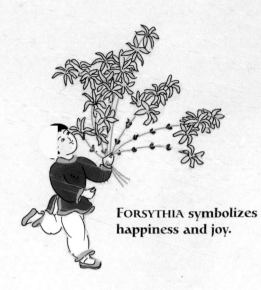

LION DANCES

For three to five days of the New Year, there are Lion Dances in front of stores to scare away evil spirits. The Lion Dances will bring good luck!

LIGHT
THE LIGHTS

The Lantern Festival is
celebrated on the 13th, 14th,
and 15th days of the new year.
This is the time to light all the
lanterns. The evil spirits are
scared away by the bright
lights of the lanterns and by
the firecrackers.

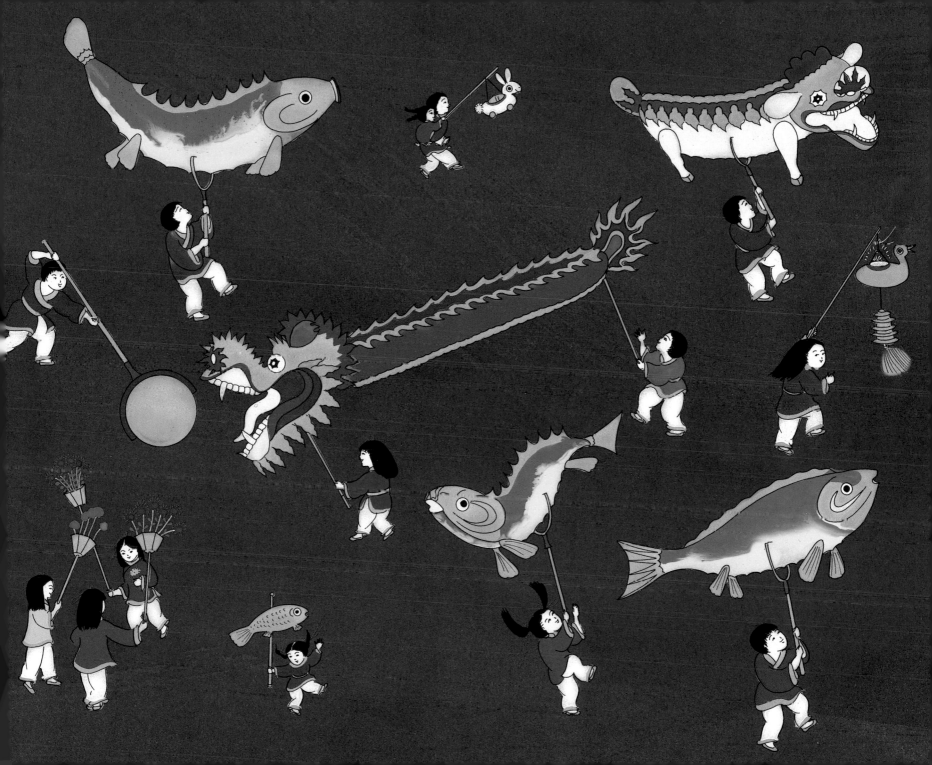

KUNG-HSI FA-TS'AI!
HAPPY NEW YEAR!

The Dragon Dances begin on New Year's Day and
last for 15 days afterward with drums and horns and happiness.
Wishing you wealth, wisdom, and power and
a wise Happy, Happy New Year!